KUNG FU TRIP

KUNG FU
TRIP

Benjamin Zephaniah

SHORTLIST

First published in 2011 by
Bloomsbury Publishing
This Large Print edition published
2011 by AudioGO Ltd
by arrangement with
Bloomsbury Publishing Plc

ISBN 978 1 405 62308 7

British Library Cataloguing in Publication Data available

Printed and bound in Great Britain by
CPI Antony Rowe, Chippenham and Eastbourne

For those who have struggled like me,
To read,
And so be free.
Sing loud and bang your drum,
For we shall overcome.

Chapter One

Leaving London

I wanted to leave London. This is why. There were too many bombs going off. After joining America in her 'war on terrorism', our Prime Minister had started his own 'war on terrorism'. Muslim houses were being raided all over the country and my Muslim friends felt as if they were under siege. I was stopped three times in one day and I don't look anything like a Muslim.

So I decided to go to China, to study kung fu at the Shaolin Temple, spiritual home of the martial arts. It would be a great trip for a kung fu fanatic like me. For all of you who do karate or judo, or any form of stick fighting, and for all of you who just watch Jackie Chan movies, this Chinese temple is where it all

1

started.

I arrived in China at 9.30 a.m. Beijing time, of course. It was exactly the same time and date that I had arrived the year before. I went to China for the first time for the same reason I had been to Russia, Lebanon, Libya, Palestine and Israel. I was sick of hearing stories about these places that were untrue—in other words propaganda—and I wanted to see these countries for myself.

When I discovered Beijing, I fell in love with the dirty, crowded city. Television had given me the idea that the city was full of millions of poor Chinese folk on bikes. Not at all. There were more cars than bikes. There were still some bicycles, but Chinese cyclists had roads of their own, many the size of British main roads.

I can never just blend in when I walk the streets in China. There are some Africans in Beijing, but there are no Rastas, so I am a bit of a novelty. Some people faint when they see me. Others take one look and run away. Children have run up to me and stroked my legs, thinking that I was a kind of big doll. Twice men have bowed down believing that I was a god.

In hotels, though, it's not the same. People in hotels don't stare so much or react in such a big way. They just ask me where I'm from, or they tell me that they have a record by someone who looks like me.

On my first day in Beijing this time round I was changing some money in the hotel when a man came up to me. He was wearing a trilby hat and a big coat, which was strange when it was so hot.

'Where you from? he asked.

'London,' I said.

'You speak Chinese?' he asked.

'No,' I said.

'You know Beijing?'

'Not very well,' I said.

'Your first time here?

'No, I've been here before,' I said.

He smiled and raised his hat. 'Ah, so you like my country?'

'Yeah man, it's cool. That's why I've come back.'

He moved closer to me and spoke quietly.

'Is everything here all right for you?'

'Yes, it's all good, man, really cool. The only thing is I know I will have a hard time finding vegan food.'

'What?' he said, tilting his hat over his eyes. 'Vegan food, no problem. We will find a place for you to get very vegan food.'

He stopped for a moment and stared into the distance. Then he looked back at me like a confused schoolboy and asked, 'What is vegan?'

'Hey,' I said, jokingly punching his shoulder, 'you're telling me that you can get me vegan food and you don't even know what vegan food is?'

I explained to him that vegan meant not eating anything that has come from an animal, so no meat, fish, milk, eggs. He said, 'Yes. Buddha.' He meant that the Buddhist restaurants in China are good for vegan food. I think they are great, some of the best in the world. They are completely vegan but on the menu you will find things like 'meat-free cow' and 'Buddha Burger'. The dishes look like meat and they taste like meat and have all the protein of meat, but without the cruelty.

Then the man with the hat said, 'I have interpreter. He speak very good English. He know all places in Beijing. He will help you.'

'No,' I said, 'it's cool. I'll be OK. I can check things out on the internet. Don't worry about me.'

'I worry about you. You are guest in my country. You are vegan guest in my country. You must enjoy your vegan stay.'

I wanted to walk away, but I didn't want to offend the guy.

'Sorry, I have to change some money,' I said, handing over two fifty-pound notes to the cashier.

He stepped aside but when I had finished and I was going up to my room, the man stopped me again.

'OK,' he said. 'You talk to my friend. He give you advice if you need, or help you with some Chinese word. He very good translator. He just make sure you all right.'

'I'm all right,' I insisted. 'I've been to Beijing before. I can get around.'

'But my friend just want to help,' he said, looking as if he was about to burst into tears.

'Does he want money?' I asked.

'No. You don't pay him if you don't like. He just give you advice, make sure you all right. If you want to use him again, maybe you give him little money. If you want him guide you around city, maybe you give him little money, but if no, it's OK. He

6

just like to meet and help foreigner.'

'What have I got to lose?' I thought. 'Where is he?' I said.

'Give me your room number.'

'No way,' I replied.

'Nothing to worry about,' he said. 'Give me your room number. He come up in ten minutes, talk with you and then go.'

I thought about it. I had never felt unsafe in China and I didn't think this guy was a crook. He was something else, but not a crook. I decided to give him my room number.

'Room 905, ninth floor.'

'OK. Ten minutes, he come.'

I went to my room and put my passport and other valuables in the safe. I sat down and began my usual thing of going through the television channels to see if they have the BBC, and then if they have any other English-speaking channels. No BBC, but I found CNN, and I cursed the management. I don't like CNN.

I was still cursing when there was a knock on the door. I looked through the spyhole and saw a woman. I thought it was housekeeping or room service so I opened the door. She walked straight past me and into the room.

'Hello, sir. Me interpreter, me city guide, me help you.'

'I thought you were going to be a man,' I said, trying not to show I was surprised.

'Me no man. Me very woman.'

She sat down on the bed. She was full of energy. Her eyes darted all over me, and all over the room.

'Where you from? What your name? How long you stay?' she asked me as quickly as a gangsta rapper, giving me no time to reply.

'Come here,' she shouted.

I walked towards her.

'Close the door,' she shouted.

I closed it.

'Sit down,' she shouted.

I sat down.

'Kiss me.'

'What?' I shouted. 'Are you crazy?'

'Kiss me now, please.'

I was lost for words. I looked around the room for help, as if someone was going to step out of a wardrobe and get me out of this.

'Kiss me,' she said again. 'You are slim, you look strong and you have hot blood.'

She pointed to the bed, she pointed to the table, she pointed to the chair, she pointed to the bathroom and she pointed to the floor.

'I want you to kiss me there, there, there, there and there. You can do that?'

I didn't know what to say.

I stood up. Then I had an idea. I was going to speak calmly and firmly. I was going to take control.

'Look, your friend—the man who approached me downstairs—said you too would be a man. He said you can speak good English and that you could help me. He said you would

9

talk to me.'

She stood up. 'You kiss me first then I talk to you. You can't just come to my country and no kiss me. I am hot chick. This is my country. Now you kiss me there, there, there, there and there. We kissy kissy, then we talky talky, you stupid man.'

I didn't want to offend the woman, but this was my room. I had rights.

'What's your name?' I asked, without knowing why.

'My name is Louise.'

'What is your Chinese name?' I like to try to use people's real names. I think it shows some respect. It's not right that African and Asian people should feel they have to make their names sound western. We should learn their names just as they learn ours.

'Shut up, just shut up and give me service.' She was getting angry. I tried to get her to speak quietly but she just got louder.

'You listen to me, dark man. We

10

kissy kissy then I take you to Tiananmen Square, and I take you to get the German food.'

I laughed.

'I don't want German food. I want vegan food.'

'My friend said you want German food.'

'No, not German, vegan. I want vegan food. How did vegan food get to be German food?'

'Never mind the food.' Now she was getting really angry. 'Look at me. You like me?'

'Yes,' I said quickly. 'You're a very nice girl.'

'So why you no kissy kissy me?'

I tried to be nice. 'I would like to get to know you first. We have only just met. You don't even know my name, and I just got off the plane. I think that if you get to know me we could be friends. I'm a poet. I have a twin sister. She's nothing like me. Do you know any kung fu?'

'Kung fu? Kung fu? Kung fu is

11

stupid. I want kissy kissy, you stupid dark man.'

She went quiet. It was a long stretch of quiet. She just stared at me and took a couple of deep breaths. Then she said, 'If you don't kissy kissy me, I will kill you.'

'That's not fair,' I said.

'If you don't kissy kissy me, I will kill you. I not afraid of dark man. I will kill you.'

'Get out,' I said. 'Get out now. Are you mad or what? You can't just come in here and say kissy kissy me. You can't just say you will kill me. What kind of woman are you? Just get out.'

She got up.

'I go,' she said. 'I will go now, and I don't need you, dark man.' And she walked out of my room.

Chapter Two

A Journey to Mongolia

It took me a while to get over the strange experience with the Chinese woman in my hotel room in Beijing. I thought about what I was going to say if I saw the man with the hat again, and deep down I was worried that the woman would come back.

*   *   *

I decided to clear my head and took a walk down to Bar Street. I like the small clubs in the side streets of the city. Most of them play hip-hop, reggae and R 'n' B. Many of the bars on Bar Street have live bands. They are probably the worst cover bands in the world, but I don't mind that. These are young kids, many come from the Philippines, dressed as punks and goths, singing Cliff Richard and Robbie Williams songs. It's their job.

What I do mind is that Bar Street is also the place where all the British tourists go. When I leave Britain, I want to get away from the beer-drinking, football-talking, party culture, me, me, me. When I'm abroad, I want to wrap myself in the local culture.

Bar Street is full of Italian, Spanish, Thai and French restaurants, which could be anywhere, but the small clubs just off the street are special. You don't pay to go in, and once you are in it's very hard to find a corner and hang cool. You have to dance.

This evening the first club I went to was half indoors and half outdoors, which brought a nice cool breeze on to the dance floor. I got myself an orange juice and stood in a corner, but within minutes two Chinese girls insisted that I dance. At first I said, 'No.'

'You're English,' said one girl.

When I asked her how she knew, she told me that English people always spend time watching before they start dancing. So trying hard not to look English, I tried dancing.

I couldn't keep up with the two girls. I could tell they had been watching Michael Jackson videos and dancing in front of the mirror. I had not, which meant I looked like a poor-performing extra in a keep-fit video.

When I could make a fool of myself no more, I left that place and visited about six more clubs before heading back to the hotel.

* * *

As I walked home, I was stopped by a group of five young Chinese people. The boys left it to the girls to speak to me.

'Where are you from?'

'England.'

15

'What is your name?'

'Benjamin.'

'Benjamin? It is a nice name. What are you doing in China?'

'I just like China.'

'So you are a tourist?'

'No, I'm not really a tourist. I have come to study kung fu.'

One of the boys took up a typical kung fu pose.

'Ah, kung fu,' he said. 'Shaolin Si.'

I knew that Si was the Chinese word for temple, and that he was saying 'Shaolin Temple'.

'Yes, Shaolin Si.'

The boy continued to speak to me in Chinese, but knowing that I couldn't understand, one of the girls translated for me.

'He said, is kung fu your job?'

'No,' I said. 'I am a poet and musician.'

Her eyes lit up. 'We are musicians. We are from Mongolia. We have been playing music here in Beijing.'

I could feel my eyes light up.

'Please, sir,' she said, 'sing a song for us.'

I tried to explain that I put poetry to music and that I wasn't really a singer.

'OK. Please, sir, will you say a poem for us?'

I chose one of my short poems and slowed it down a bit. It looked as if the two girls understood much of what I was saying but the boys just liked the rhythm.

When I finished, they clapped frantically and thanked me.

'No problem,' I said and I began to say goodbye.

'No, please,' said the girl. 'Please wait. We play Mongolian music for you.'

Quickly they took instruments from their backpacks and began to play. The music was beautiful. The noise of the traffic around me just disappeared and I felt like I was with them in Mongolia. I thanked them and began to say goodnight again when the girl spoke.

'No, sir, please wait. We sing Mongolian song for you.'

'You just did,' I said.

'No,' she said. 'That was just music. Now we do song with music.'

Then they began to play again and the two girls began to sing. Now this really was heaven. I was rooted to the spot. I could see that it was very important for them to share their music with me, but, as I listened, I wondered if they knew how much their playing meant to me. After the bombs in London, the long flight and the strange kissy kissy woman, this was just what I needed. When the music was over, I hugged them goodbye and I felt like I floated back to my hotel.

Chapter Three

Kung Fu

I went to bed early that night but woke up the next morning at 4 a.m. Jet lag.

I remember when I first started travelling, I just couldn't understand what jet lag was. When I arrived in a country, I just tuned into the time of that country, and when I got home I did the same. But as I got older things started to change and it would take me days, and sometimes weeks, to adjust to different time zones. I hate jet lag, and here I was again looking at the ceiling and wondering what to do. I tried just lying still and keeping my eyes closed as I counted sheep, then trees, clouds, traffic wardens and blades of grass.

I opened my eyes, reached for the TV remote control and tried all the channels until I stopped at the English-speaking station of CCTV, China's state-run TV channel. I liked this channel; there was never a critical word of the government but I really enjoyed watching the way the Chinese reported things to do with Britain and the USA. Much of the coverage was rubbish, but much of what we get to hear about China is also rubbish, so for a while I watched the CCTV news and, in my mind, compared rubbish with rubbish. It was all rubbish, just different kinds of rubbish. Television news all stinks.

*　　　*　　　*

At last morning proper came and I began to hear movement out on the streets and around the hotel, so I decided to put on my running gear and go down to the gym.

The hotel brochure had a wonderful photo of the gym that was on the second floor, but the lift wouldn't take me there. I pressed the button marked 2 but the lift went past it and stopped at level 1. So I pressed 2 again and it went up, passing 2 and stopping at 3. This happened a few times so I went to the reception.

'It's really weird,' I said to the receptionist. 'I want to go to the gym but the lift won't go there. It goes to the third and first floors, but it won't go to the second, and there are no stairs.'

'We don't have a gym here,' she said, to my surprise.

'No gym? What you talking about, no gym? There is a gym. It's on the second floor. I saw it in the brochure.'

'Oh, I'm sorry. There was a gym, sir, but the gym is closed and it will be closed for the next six months, and because the gym is closed, sir, the lift will not stop at the second floor.'

I was furious, but tried to keep calm.

'Closed? Why didn't you say so before? If I knew you had no gym when I was choosing a hotel, I wouldn't have come here. The reason why I picked this hotel was because you had a gym. This is terrible. I have to exercise, I have to. It makes me who I am. It's part of who I am. And if I don't exercise I'll get fat, and you won't like me when I'm fat.'

'I'm sorry, sir. The gym will be closed for six months.'

I realised that I was not going to get anywhere arguing with the receptionist so I went to my room and wrote an email to Lorrimer, my travel agent and my Mr Fix Things back in London.

Dear Lorrimer,
I have arrived in Beijing and I am well, but there is a problem. There is no gym at the hotel. Well, there is

22

one but I am told that it will be closed for a long time and so I won't be able to use it. I'm really upset, man, as you know I picked this place because it said it had a gym, and now I'm stuck here. I don't think there's anything that can be done now but I thought I should let you know.

Have a good play,

Benjamin

Later that day I received an email from Lorrimer.

Dear Benjamin,
Sorry about the mix-up. I have sorted it out for you. The gym is closed but the manager Mr Woo has given you permission to use the gym as much as you like. If there is a problem, just ask for him.
    I hope you enjoy the rest of your stay. Do let me know if there is

anything else that I can do for you.

All the best,

Lorrimer

I was told that I could get to the gym by using the fire escape, so I ran down from the ninth floor. When I arrived, there were seven people there to welcome me. I was shown to the gym and it wasn't a gym. It was a swimming pool with some exercise equipment around it.

'Is this it?' I asked Shirley, real name Zhao Bin, who was leader of the group of people who began to follow me around.

'Yes,' she replied. 'This is very special, just for you.'

Now get this. I step on to the running machine and all seven of them stood and watched me. Some of them were watching how my feet connected to the treadmill; others were clocking the meters showing my speed; and others were studying my forehead to see how much I was sweating. These people followed me to the small weights machine and watched me exercising my forearms, my chest muscles, my thighs and my hamstrings. I was amazed at their level of interest.

Then I saw something at the far side of the swimming pool that really got me excited—a punch speed bag and a pair of boxing gloves.

'Zhao Bin,' I said to Shirley, 'can I have a go on that?'

'Yes,' she said, 'no problem, everything here is for you. Mr Woo say you can have access to anything. Let's go.'

I ran round to the speed bag with my followers walking quickly behind me, then I put the gloves on and began to punch the boxing bag. They were now like excited school kids, shouting 'Wow!' as I connected with the bag. As I built up my work rate and really began to move around the bag, bobbing and weaving, they shouted words of encouragement like, 'Very good', 'You are strong' and 'Powerful!'

I would box for a while and then stop for a rest. Every time I stopped someone took a towel and wiped my face, another person would put a bottle of water to my mouth, while someone else wiped the sweat from my upper body. They had become my ringside team.

After six three-minute rounds I gave up boxing and decided to end with a bit of kung fu. I stood still and straight. I concentrated and focused my eyes directly in front of me. I breathed in deeply, and out, and in, and as I breathed out again I began the form. When you do a form, you have to concentrate and nothing must distract you. I'm normally good at all that, but this time I had people cheering and making strange noises at me. I stayed focused and when I had finished I had a loud round of applause that embarrassed me.

'You very good,' said one member of the crowd.

'You know kung fu?' I asked him.

'No,' he replied. 'You are master. I will learn from you.'

'I am no master. After I leave Beijing I will be going to meet the real master for some training. He's a real master, not me,' I told him.

'Where is your master?' he asked.

'Shaolin Temple,' I said.

He screamed, 'Shaolin Temple! You go Shaolin Temple?' That grabbed the attention of the others.

'He is going to Shaolin Temple,' he told them, and then they all bowed down as if to worship me.

Although most people think of kung fu when they think of China, the truth is that most of the people in China don't do kung fu. The Chinese know that kung fu is an important part of their culture but most don't have time for it, which is why they have great respect for foreigners like me who are trying to keep it alive. They were even more impressed by my forthcoming journey to the Shaolin Temple. Even the Chinese who do take up kung fu do it at the local gym and won't bother to train high up a mountain where it's either really hot or really cold.

They lined up for me, and as I walked down the line like a royal person or a general inspecting troops each of them shook my hand and thanked me for the demonstration, wishing me good luck and prosperity. When I had promised that I would report back to them after my trip, I was shown to the fire escape by Zhao Bin and made my way to my room to do a bit of writing on my new novel, *Teacher's Dead*. It's a novel for teenagers, an easy read about a kid who kills his teacher. Just kidding. It's not really easy; just my way of dealing with it.

Chapter Four

Who Am I?

This was the big day. I was going to the Shaolin Temple to meet the kung fu master.

I got up after a night of very little sleep and opened the curtains. It was as if the sun was waiting behind the curtains. It slapped me across my face and blinded me for a few seconds, then it sent a wave of heat through my body, reminding me that I was away from home, on another continent.

*　　　*　　　*

I had always found it very difficult to understand how an economy grows. My visit to China changed all that. As I looked out of the window, I saw high-rise buildings that weren't there when I went to bed. Hundreds of vehicles were delivering building materials, and thousands more were taking people to work. Everywhere I looked it was the same. China's economy was expanding OK, and I was watching it. I was standing on it, it was growing underneath my feet. As I stood there looking at China developing all around me, I wondered if anyone was watching me, and if so what they would make of the naked Rastaman on the ninth floor scratching his chest and feeling the future.

*   *   *

I made my way to reception to check out. As I was trying to leave, I saw out of the corner of my eye a hand reaching for my suitcase. I slapped the hand and pushed the person away with my bottom. He fell over and struggled like a cockroach on its back.

'What are you up to? You messed with my bag, guy.'

Well, I could see he wasn't a real criminal. He was too scared.

'Benjamin?' he said. 'Are you Benjamin?'

I was surprised.

'How do you know my name?'

'Me your driver,' he replied. 'Me come to take you to the airport.'

'I'm sorry,' I said. 'You should have introduced yourself. If I see a hand going for my bag, I do my kung fu.'

'That is not kung fu,' he said.

I reached out and gave him a hand up from the floor.

'That's kung fu all right. It's called Afro Botty style and it floored you, didn't it?'

'Afro Botty style,' he said, looking at my bottom. 'Where did you learn this style?'

'It is an ancient African martial art that was developed by a great voodoo master who fought with giant big-eared elephants.' I was joking, of course.

'Very good,' he said. 'Are you ready to go now?'

*   *   *

The driver's name was Mr Young. He drove the way I like my drivers to drive, fast but safe, and he loved talking.

'Mr Lorrimer tell me that you are famous man in London.'

'Not really,' I said. 'I write poems and sometimes I go on television.'

'So you are rich and have many wives?'

'No. I'm not rich and I don't have many wives. I don't even have one wife.'

'You are going to Shaolin Temple?' he asked.

'Yes.'

'Why?'

'Kung fu,' I said.

He misunderstood me.

'Very good. You are going to teach

Chinese monk ancient African martial art of the Afro Botty style. Great, very great. Will make Chinese monk very happy and make giant big-eared elephants fall over, like me.'

I laughed. 'Yeah, like you.'

I was worried. I had told him this crazy stuff about the Afro Botty style and at the time I thought that he knew I was joking, but I could see now that he was taking it very seriously. I didn't know if I should tell him that I was only joking or just let it go, but then he made it harder for me.

We stopped outside the airport terminal and before I got out, he said, 'These monks at the temple are a bit old-fashioned. They think that good things come only from China. They think that China is the centre of the world. They are always taking about this Chinese style and that Chinese style. It will be very good if you go there and teach them the ancient art of the African Afro Botty style. Good luck.' He was being so nice and serious I decided not to tell him I'd been pulling his leg.

*   *   *

I had never taken an internal flight in China before so I was nervous, because it seemed like every time I heard the words 'Chinese airline' it was to do with a plane crash on a remote mountain that couldn't be reached for two days. But the plane I boarded was new, newer than Mr Young's car. Every seat had its own TV screen, radio headphones, and a little box full of crackers, boiled sweets and a bottle of mineral water from the mountains of Shandong. It was great.

I sat in my window seat on the plane and started playing with the gadgets like a little boy with a new PlayStation. The two seats next to me were empty but as soon as we'd taken off and levelled out a man came and sat next to me.

'I know you,' he said.

'You've been to England?' I replied.

'No, but I know you. You are famous.'

'Well, a little famous. So you've seen me on television?'

'That's right. I've seen you on television. You are great. When I see you, I always say to my wife and children, "That man is a great man." Yes, I know you. You are like a prophet. You are a leader of people.'

I was beginning to feel embarrassed by his words, and was trying hard to think what to say next when his eyes lit up.

'Please,' he said, 'can I have your autograph?'

'Of course.'

He went to his seat a few rows behind me and came back with a postcard with a picture of the Great Wall on it. He turned it over and said, 'Sign, please.'

I signed it and handed it back to him with a smile. He took it with a smile that quickly changed when he saw my autograph.

'What is this?' he said, looking confused.

'My autograph,' I replied, also looking confused.

'What? You are not Bob Marley?' he questioned me angrily.

'I didn't say I was,' I replied angrily.

'You said you're famous. You said you've been on television.'

'I have.'

'Are you famous?'

'I wouldn't say I'm famous, I'd say I'm well known.'

He looked more hopeful.

'So you're famous. What for? Are you actor or singer?'

'I'm a poet.'

He looked disappointed. He threw the card back at me.

'Poet? You are a poet? Who ever heard of a famous poet that is alive?

There is no such thing. You may think you're famous but you just waste my time.'

'Look,' I said, 'I didn't come to China to be famous and I don't care if I'm famous, but you don't have to be dead to be famous, and I'm sorry to have to tell you this, but Bob Marley is dead.'

'He is not dead,' he said.

'His music lives on and his spirit is still with us, but his body has gone.'

'Are you serious?'

'Yes, he died a long time ago.'

He looked at me for what felt like a lifetime. It made me feel uncomfortable. The more he looked at me, the more it looked as if he was going to cry. Then he walked away. I didn't even have time to read the list of ingredients on my packet of crackers when he came back with another postcard. This one had a picture of the Forbidden City on it. He handed it to me and said, 'Please, I want Bob Marley's autograph.'

'He's no longer with us,' I said.

'I understand, but you must do Bob Marley's autograph for me.'

I pointed to the card with my pen and checked that my hearing was in working order.

'Let me get this right. You want me to sign this not with my name, but with Bob Marley's name?'

'Yes.'

I thought about it for a moment and I decided that to sign it was not a great sin. I wasn't asking for any money, and I was sure Bob would have done it for me, so I signed the card as Bob Marley and handed it back to the man. He was happy again. He was still looking at the card as he walked back to his seat.

'Thank you,' he said. 'This is very good; very, very good. I like this, but poetry is rubbish.'

Chapter Five

The Airport

As the plane landed safely, the passengers clapped the pilots. When I see and hear this, it always amazes me because I know that most planes are landed by computer. I remember being in the cockpit of a plane in East Africa once and when it landed the passengers clapped the pilots while the pilots clapped the computer. I wondered if the pilots of this Chinese aeroplane were doing the same.

My taxi picked me up and, after driving for an hour, we arrived at the hotel in the town of Dengfeng. Dengfeng could easily have been one of those small Chinese towns in the middle of nowhere. The kind that white people never see unless they have a film crew in tow, but this place is special, and what makes it so is the Shaolin Temple.

This town is the last stop before you ascend the mountains to the temple, so the people of Dengfeng have become used to seeing groups of foreigners. Some of the shops are named after the temple even though they may not sell anything to do with the martial arts. Chinese youngsters dressed in their kung fu suits can be seen jogging through the streets, and it's hot, really hot.

*　　　*　　　*

My hotel was trying very hard to be modern and international. At first it looked fine. Painted on the bright white walls of the reception area were figures of kung fu fighters in action. Woven into the carpet on the floor was the yin and yang symbol. This symbolises hard and soft, male and female. Yin and yang are the symbols of unity and harmony used by martial artists all over the world.

The first thing I noticed when the hotel porter opened the door of my room was a strong smell of urine coming from the bathroom. It was the kind of smell you can get in telephone boxes.

I put my head into the bathroom and sniffed hard so that the porter would notice. He smiled and said, 'Very good.'

'Erm,' I said, 'there is a strange smell. Can you smell it?'

'Very good,' he said.

'No. Not very good. Bad smell.' I pointed into the toilet.

'Yes,' he said, 'very good.'

We stepped further into my hotel room. I could feel my shoes sinking into the carpet. It was so soaked that it felt as if it had been on a pub crawl in Newcastle on a Saturday night. The wallpaper looked as if it was trying to leave the room. The room itself smelt like a farm.

'It stinks,' I declared.

'Yes, it stinks. Very good for you.'

When things get lost in translation, I never think I am better because the other person doesn't understand English. Even if somebody has only a few words of English I rate them higher than me. After all, I only know three words in Chinese and one of them is a really rude one. But I was annoyed because the smell in the room was so bad.

The porter left, and I unpacked my suitcase and plugged in my laptop. One of the things about Chinese hotels is that they all seem to have free internet access. I logged on and sent an email to everyone who cared, telling them that I had arrived and things were looking good but smelling a little weird.

I surfed the internet for a couple of hours to read up on the news back home. Then, when darkness fell, I thought I would take my nostrils for a walk in the fresh air. It was a Chinese national holiday and the very young and the very old were out on the streets enjoying the warm summer night.

As usual, people stared at me, because I stood out from the crowd. In this town they were used to seeing foreigners, but not foreigners like me. I loved the attention. In all my travels in China I had never felt unsafe, and I had never been insulted. If I stared back, they stared more, but I soon discovered that if I smiled they smiled too, so that's what I did and I found that it was a lovely way to greet their curiosity.

Just down the road from the hotel I came across one of those classic Chinese sights. It reminded me of the China that I used to see on television, the China that shows the world that great things are possible if you work together and embrace collective spirit. In a large square in front of a shopping centre, I saw about two hundred people of all ages. They were all dancing the same steps in unison to Chinese pop music. The music was terrible, but the dancing was good.

The oldest person I saw looked over a hundred years old, but she glided through the movements. As I looked at her I thought, 'I hope I can do that when I'm her age, and I wonder if I can do that to a Fat Boy Slim tune?'

I soon learnt that watching was just as rewarding as dancing, so I looked on and all my troubles just melted away.

Chapter Six

Zen and the Art of Breathing

Once again I slept very little and I was awake early the next morning. As I lay on my back and stretched, I opened my eyes and saw a pair of kung fu fighters painted on to the ceiling above me.

'Wow!' I said aloud.

Ever since I was a young boy images of kung fu had inspired me to practise. When I left the cinema after watching martial arts films, I would kick and punch my way down the street. If I watched a film at home, as soon as it was over I would push the furniture aside and practise the moves I had just seen. Now, when I saw the fighting men above me I was energised once more, threw back the blankets and jumped out of bed. As I jumped, the blankets got tangled with my feet and I fell over. I looked up to the fighting men and laughed.

'You two, you tricked me,' I said, and then I reached up and untangled my feet.

I stayed on the floor and did twenty press-ups, I turned and did fifty crunches, and then I ran on the spot for fifteen minutes.

After I had showered and dressed I took an envelope from my computer case. Back in London my Shifu (that's the Chinese word for teacher) had given me this important envelope which contained vital information. Inside, on one sheet of paper was the name Zhang Yanli and a phone number. I had been advised to contact her as soon as I got to Dengfeng. On the second piece of paper, written in Chinese, were notes for the teacher about my level of kung fu and the type of training that I needed. Growing numbers of tourists were visiting the Shaolin

Temple, and many kung fu teachers were beginning to charge students high prices for poor teaching. So the second paper also made it clear that I was to be introduced to a top-quality teacher.

I called Zhang Yanli. Less than an hour later she was knocking on my door. She was in her early thirties and full of smiles. She looked like a school teacher with sensible shoes, sensible glasses and a skirt two inches below the knee, carrying an old-fashioned leather briefcase. I felt the way I used to feel when I saw my biology teacher. She said I could call her Yvonne, but I insisted on calling her by her Chinese name, so she said I should call her Yanli.

I handed Yanli the paper containing the notes and we left the hotel straight away. We got a taxi, and as we reached the outskirts of Dengfeng we started to drive up a steep hill. The hill got steeper and steeper, and the town with its busy

47

shops and eating places soon gave way to a twisting road with kung fu schools on both sides. I asked Yanli if the taxi could stop, and I spent ten minutes watching about three hundred young kung fu students as they practised their form.

Forms are sets of kung fu kicks, punches and stances, strung together to make one long sequence. They are hard work. The moves must be done in a very precise way. The timing must be perfect. Even the breathing has to be done in a controlled way. I knew a few forms, but the biggest class I had been to had about forty students, so when I saw so many students all working together I was inspired. A Shifu (teacher) high up on a platform would shout instructions. At the shout three hundred fists shot forward; another shout and three hundred feet kicked high; another shout and three hundred bodies would leap into the air, kick, spin and land on the ground. Then, as they landed on their sides, all the students would kick out again. I wanted some of that.

'Take me to the master,' I said to Yanli, and we continued on our way.

*   *   *

When we reached the gateway to the temple grounds, I was shown a huge statue of Bodhidharma. He is the man who is said to have started kung fu as we know it today, and he is also the founder of Zen Buddhism. I've met a lot of great people in my time on Earth, and I've read about many others, so I really mean it when I say that I believe that Bodhidharma was one of the greatest people that ever lived, and I'm not a Buddhist.

Bodhidharma was born in India, the son of a great king. He himself could have been king but he was interested in higher things. He left India and went on a journey to find enlightenment. It's quite ironic that he left India for that purpose, when so many people now go to India to find their spiritual home. The traveller was not seen for many years until he got to China in the year AD 527. He met with the Emperor Wu Ti but they did not agree about Buddhism, so Bodhidharma went north.

There are lots of stories about Bodhidharma and here's one.

On his way north Bodhidharma came to a great river. He had to cross it, but there were no boats. All he could see was an old woman on the riverbank, minding her own business. Bodhidharma noticed that she had a bundle of reeds so he politely asked her for one. She gave it to him and he placed it on the water, stood on it and sailed across the river. OK, it's not the same as walking across the water, but it's still not that easy.

The emperor had sent someone to

follow Bodhidharma. When he got to the river, he had the same problem, so he went to the woman and took a handful of reeds from her without asking, tied them together, put them on the water and stood on them. He sank.

When the man got out of the water, he said to the woman, 'How does that work? He does it on one reed, but I take a bunch of reeds and I almost drown.'

'It's easy,' replied the woman. 'He asked politely. He had manners, so it worked for him. You just came up and stole my reeds so you should not expect the same results. Now dry yourself off and go hire a boat.'

And here's another amazing story about Bodhidharma. When he died, his body was put in a cave and there was great mourning all over the Buddhist world. A man from the government called Songyun had been away on a mission and knew nothing about the great man's death.

On his way back from his mission, Songyun saw Bodhidharma walking towards the west. He was barefoot with one shoe in his hand.

Songyun asked Bodhidharma where he was going and Bodhidharma replied, 'I'm going to paradise.' Songyun thought it was a joke. There was good music in the west, and the weather was good, but it could never be called paradise. When Songyun got back, he insisted that he had seen Bodhidharma so the emperor made an order that the tomb be opened. When they opened the tomb, it was empty, all except for one shoe.

*   *   *

So now in kung fu and Buddhist shops all over the world you can buy little statues and dolls of Bodhidharma sailing on a single reed or walking with one shoe in his hand.

When Bodhidharma got to the Shaolin Temple, the monks were practising Buddhism by reading books, chanting and praying aloud. That wasn't for Bodhidharma, though. Instead, he wanted to promote Zen Buddhism, which simply means silent or still Buddhism. He believed that it was better to be silent.

To help his Chinese students to understand this, Bodhidharma gave them yoga exercises. The most important of these was sitting cross-legged in the lotus position. At first the Chinese thought this would be easy, until they realised that you need to be very fit to sit still for such a long time. Bodhidharma was smart. I'm putting this in my own words now, but this is what he said.

'OK, it is too difficult for you to sit still, so I will give you moving yoga. This will help you to get fit and use your breath in a yogic way. Now copy me.'

Then he taught them a series of movements similar to t'ai chi. Later he added more movements based on the way animals move. When the emperor ordered his troops to kill all the monks in the temple, Bodhidharma made his students speed up their movements to defend themselves. This led to the creation of kung fu, where fighting isn't the most important thing: the most important thing is self-awareness.

*   *   *

Now that's all well and good. In fact I think that's amazing, but that's not why I think Bodhidharma is the greatest human ever to walk the planet. This is why I really think he's great. He converted the whole of China and beyond to Zen Buddhism without preaching or standing on a soapbox, without any helpers, and he didn't have anything like the Bible or the Koran or the Torah to spread his message.

Bodhidharma was just an ugly bloke who never shouted his beliefs. He liked being on his own, and it is said that he lived in a cave for nine years. When people came to him for help, he told them to stop looking out at other people or up towards the sky. He told them to look inside themselves. He told them to listen to their breath. He told them that through silence they could find the truth.

So as I stood in the temple grounds and looked up at the statue and looked down at the shops selling Bodhidharma cups, baseball caps, key rings, watches and T-shirts, I couldn't help but wonder what he would make of it all. It was so commercial.

Chapter Seven

Watching the Monks

When our taxi reached the grounds of the temple, my guide Yanli just waved her hand and we were let through the gates, unlike the crowds of tourists who had to queue and pay. Then I saw the building that I had dreamt of seeing for so long, the Shaolin Temple. I had arrived at a place that was thousands of kilometres from my home, but it was a place that seemed completely familiar.

*   *   *

The taxi stopped and we got out. I walked away to admire the temple on my own. Tourists were taking photos and stallholders were selling their wares. I felt great. Then I had one of those moments when you feel that there is someone else with you. For a moment I wondered if it was the spirit of Bodhidharma himself.

I looked around to find a man standing right behind me. He was dressed just like they dress in classic kung fu films. He was wearing a long fancy gown over a satin kung fu suit. The gown—covered in embroidery —looked very heavy but very beautiful. The man was in his mid-thirties. His beard left his chin like a dark icicle, ending in a perfect point at his waist. His delicate moustache hugged the top of his lip as if it was painted on, then crawled down the side of his chin in the same direction as his beard. It had a lot of catching up to do.

'You have come to learn more about kung fu?' he said. I recognised his accent.

'Hey, you're from Birmingham,' I said. 'Me too. I studied karate at temple school. Did you?'

'I don't need to study,' the man said sternly. 'My style of fighting is the art of fighting without thinking.'

'That's good,' I replied. 'Very Zen. So are you from Birmingham or what?'

'This is my home. That place you call Birmingham was just a pit stop on my earthly journey. Why have you come here?' he asked, looking as if he didn't approve of me.

'I've wanted to see the temple since I was small. I grew up watching all those kung fu films in Birmingham, and I am sick of learning second-rate kung fu, so I came here for the real thing.'

'Oh,' he said loudly, 'let me tell you something. There is also lots of rubbish kung fu here. It is hard to find the good kung fu here, but I can teach you.'

'I already have a teacher,' I said.

'Who is he?'

I pointed towards Yanli and said, 'I don't know who the teacher is but she's taking me to him.'

'Don't trust her,' he said. 'She will take you to nowhere, where the teachers teach you nothing.'

'Do you know her?' I asked.

'I know her kind.'

His words reminded me of the many times people have come up to me in the street, or on a train or a bus, and told me that they are poets. I never write off such people outright, but I do ask myself if they are a mad person or a genius. I have come across both.

I was rescued by a shout from Yanli.

'Benjamin, let's go.'

'So your mother and father gave you the name Benjamin?' the man asked.

'I have to go,' I said.

'You don't have to do anything, but you must never do nothing,' he said.

'I'm sure you're right in your own way,' I replied.

'Remember, the good kung fu is

here. I was taught by Bruce Lee and I know the secret of the art of the smelly finger. I can set free your thing. Remember me, my name is Fat Thumb. I was given that name by the big balloon. Fat Thumb.'

This was weird. 'Thanks, Fat Thumb. If my thing needs to be set free, I'll come back,' I said, and I went back to the taxi.

* * *

We drove up a bumpy, half-made road that ran along the outer wall of the temple and arrived at a large open square with houses on all sides. We walked up to one of the houses. Yanli shouted and two very young boys came out wearing yellow robes. They smiled and bowed. I smiled and bowed. You know that you're getting old when the monks look younger than you.

I was invited to come in and sit down with a series of hand gestures.

The place looked as untidy as most student flats, with plates of leftover food on a table and half-full cups everywhere. The television was blasting out a kung fu film at full volume.

We had just sat down when another monk walked in, wearing orange robes. Everyone stood up on his arrival, and so did I. Yanli introduced me and told me that this man was the abbot. We bowed. People made room for the abbot to take the best seat in front of the television, and then we sat down to watch the kung fu film.

*　　*　　*

So there I was. I had arrived at the great Shaolin Temple. I had met the monks and the abbot, and what were we doing? Watching kung fu films made in Hong Kong about Shaolin monks fighting off really ugly bad guys with black teeth who had come to steal their ancient secrets. All that was missing was the clumsy English voice-over, a part of kung fu films that I always enjoy.

One of the monks made some tea, and after that he then made sure my cup was never empty.

As we sat in a semicircle, eyes glued to the TV, the monks would speak to each other in Chinese, but I knew they were talking about me because every now and then I would hear my name.

Yanli then made a call on her mobile phone and soon another monk turned up at the house. This older monk was full of energy. He shook my hand and greeted me as if he knew me. Yanli spoke to him for a short time and then she turned to me.

'This is Shifu Li Guofu,' she said. 'He will be your teacher. You can call him Iron Breath.'

'Shifu Iron Breath,' I said aloud.

'No, just Iron Breath,' said Yanli.

'Does he speak English?' I asked.

'No,' she replied. 'He doesn't need to. Language will only get in the way.'

We started to discuss the fee and once again I was made aware of the fact that I couldn't speak Chinese. I just let Yanli and Iron Breath talk to each other while I tried to look as if I knew what was being said. At last Yanli spoke to me.

'He wants nine thousand yuan.'

'Nine thousand yuan?' I exclaimed, and everyone looked at me.

I took out my money converter to work it out. Nine thousand yuan was about six hundred pounds, which meant that my fourteen lessons would cost more than forty pounds each. I began to do some quick thinking. It would be great to have my own Shaolin monk, but it did seem like a lot of money.

'It's too much,' I said to Yanli.

She spoke to Iron Breath again and then to me.

'He said if you really want him to teach you, you will pay his price.'

'But I don't even know how good he is,' I said.

She spoke to him for a while and then everyone else in the room stood up and went outside to the courtyard.

Iron Breath spoke to Yanli and then she said, 'Iron Breath said you must hit him.'

'Me?'

'Yes, hit him using your hands and your feet. You can hit him anywhere but his face.'

Iron Breath nodded and I took my place in front of him. To try to catch him out I suddenly aimed a punch at his stomach, but he just breathed in enough for me to miss him. I then tried a kick to his knee, and he lifted it as if in slow motion so that I fell forward. I managed to stay on my feet and tried a back-spinning kick, but he just laughed as he sidestepped it.

'Wait,' said Yanli.

I stopped. Iron Breath breathed in and out deeply three times, fixing his gaze in front of him.

'OK,' said Yanli. 'You can hit him now, anywhere you like, even his head, but not in his face.'

He raised his arms above his head and I punched him in his stomach and my fist just bounced back at me. I kicked him in his ribs and his thighs, chopped him in his neck and punched him in the back of his head, and he just kept looking in front of him. Nothing moved him, but my hands and feet were suffering.

'Stand back,' said Yanli.

I stood back and all the other young monks ran to Iron Breath and started to punch and kick him. He did not move an inch. When they had finished the attack, one of the monks handed me a wooden table leg.

'Hit him on his head as hard as you like,' said Yanli.

'Are you mad?' I said. 'I can't hit him with this, it's so hard.'

'Hit him,' she said. 'With all the strength you have, or he will make you do it twice.'

I took the chair leg. He leant forward and I jumped as high as I could and hit his head with all the power I had in me. The leg broke, but Iron Breath raised his head and winked at me. Then he began to walk away.

'Where's he going?' I shouted.

'He thinks you don't like him so he is going. You think he's not worth it,' said Yanli.

'No. I mean yes,' I shouted. 'He's worth it OK. There's absolutely no problem at all. I'll pay him what he wants.'

She called him back and we became friends again.

Chapter Eight

All in the Mind

Iron Breath turned up at my hotel later that afternoon. I handed him nine thousand yuan in a plain brown envelope and we pushed the bed against a wall, giving us just enough space to practise.

After the warm-up stretches he began to do the movements and I followed him. The stances were low, and low stances hurt, but learning how to do the moves while you are in the stances is what really pushes you to the limits. There were times when I wanted to cry because of the pain but he didn't understand English so when I said 'Can I have a rest?' or 'I think I'm gonna die,' he just carried on. Soon I realised that I just had to go with it. After all, I was paying big pounds for it.

*   *   *

There isn't a word for kung fu in English. The nearest you can get is 'hard work' or 'dedication'. You could also call it concentration. Kung fu is about the way you use your mind. Martial arts is the fighting bit. Learning punches and kicks is just one part of kung fu, and some say the easiest, which is why kung fu has the highest drop-out rate of any sport. Many people watch a couple of Bruce Lee films and want to do the fighting, but when it comes to the non-fighting part they drop out because it isn't easy.

*   *   *

There were times in my session with Iron Breath when I just couldn't work out how to do a move. It was at these times that you could see the difference in teaching methods

68

between east and west. In the west, if you are doing a move that you cannot get right the teacher will get you to do it over and over again. In China, when you are having problems the teacher will ask you to stop, sit down and go through it in your mind.

The first time Iron Breath asked me to do this I was trying to do a difficult move which involved tricky hand, foot and twisting movements. When he saw that I was struggling to do all this at the same time, he sat down and, copying him, so did I. Then he pointed to his head and closed his eyes, and then he pointed to my head. I realised that he wanted me to think about the form. I did, and when I stood up I just seemed to float through the movements. This approach has changed the way I train ever since.

*　　　*　　　*

We trained for two hours and by the end I was pouring with sweat and in desperate need of the comfort of my mother, but I knew that I had a great teacher in Iron Breath. We set a time for our next lessons—twelve o'clock every day—then he left and I fell asleep.

Chapter Nine

The Art of Long Tongue

I was continuing to lose the fight against jet lag. I woke up at 10 p.m. and I wasn't able to get to sleep again until six in the morning, only to be woken up by Iron Breath knocking at my door at midday. I felt as if I had just finished one kung fu lesson, had a snooze and started another one. The second session was harder than the first one. Iron Breath added more moves and he also added an hour to the time. It was hard, sweaty and painful, but I loved it.

*   *   *

I called Yanli and we agreed to meet later and look for a vegan restaurant. With a couple of hours to spare before our meeting I went for another walk. As always I did what I loved doing most, strolling through the tiny back streets.

Everywhere I walked I was stared at. Women would run indoors to tell other women to come out and see me, men would shout names at me like Eddie Murphy and Denzel Washington, and one man even called me Kofi Annan—the ex-Secretary-General of the United Nations.

I went into a supermarket and business stopped as all the extremely young staff just followed me around, watching as I tried to read the contents on packets. I saw some fruit that I wanted, so I went to get me some. Suddenly there was a rush towards me, and everyone wanted to help. I settled for five helpers and the others watched. They made life so easy for me. I would point to the fruits I needed, a girl would pick them up, another girl checked that they were OK. She would then hand them to a boy who put them into a bag that was being held by another boy. Person number five was an older girl who seemed to be telling the rest what to do. They all looked happy to help me. True service with a smile.

I stepped out of the supermarket to find that it was pouring with rain, which was welcome because it seemed to clear the polluted air. There didn't seem to be any kind of controls on vehicle emissions. A couple of times I saw exhaust fumes that were so black I couldn't see what they were coming out of.

*   *   *

Yanli came to my hotel later with good news.

'It was difficult but I have found one vegan restaurant. It's run by women and it's open right now,' she said.

'Hey, that sounds like my kind of

place,' I said, rubbing my hands together and licking my lips.

*   *   *

It did turn out to be my kind of place, although I had never seen anywhere quite like it. The restaurant was attached to a temple called the Yong Tai Temple, which was very close to the Shaolin Temple.

Yong Tai Temple was built in AD 521. Princess Yong Tai lived, fought and studied kung fu there. She insisted on being treated like the other nuns, but when she left they renamed it after her. To this day nuns live in the temple and unlike so many others that have turned into tourist attractions, this is still a place of worship.

Most tourists go to Shaolin, so two visitors like us, who were willing to spend a bit of money, were very welcome. The food was wonderful, and before we left I bought a few souvenirs. I didn't need or want them but I wanted to help the temple.

On the way back we went back to the Shaolin Temple. It was getting late but I needed to get to know my spiritual home.

When we arrived, most of the tourists had gone, and the stallholders were packing up and leaving. I took a photo of the front of the temple and Yanli and I headed for the entrance, where we found a middle-aged monk eating a pizza.

'Can we go in?' I asked.

'No. Closed,' he said, shaking his head.

'We just want a quick look around.'

'Sorry. Closed,' he said, filling up on pizza.

Then he noticed Yanli next to me and jumped to attention. They spoke to each other excitedly and then he waved us in.

'What happened then?' I asked.

'Oh, nothing. He's just an old

friend. I haven't seen him for some time. He's a serious monk now but he used to be a club DJ in Shanghai.'

'Are you joking?'

'No, I'm serious,' she said. 'He was called DJ Long Tongue.'

'DJ Long Tongue. So why Long Tongue?'

'Because he's always had this thing about pizzas, and when he was working the stereo decks he used to hold a piece of pizza in his mouth and it looked like he had a long pizza tongue.'

It was good for a laugh but I didn't believe her.

'Very funny, and I suppose he played at the Ministry of Sound?'

'Almost. He was booked but he couldn't get a visa. I know it sounds crazy but it's true. Anyway, he says we've got an hour. Let's get moving.'

Chapter Ten

The Shaolin Temple

Shaolin Temple was built in AD 495 and became the centre of Buddhist learning in China. When Bodhidharma first came to the temple in AD 540, the monks would not let him in as they thought he was just a passing tourist. Even back then, tourists were trying to get in. Bodhidharma went instead to a nearby cave, where it is said that he meditated for nine years. He meditated so much that he didn't notice when birds built a nest on his shoulder, and his shadow became embedded in the cave wall. The nest has gone but it is said his shadow is still there now. When he came down from the cave, the monks let him in at last.

Today the temple is one of the

busiest in China, so I was feeling quite chuffed at having a private tour.

I had expected one big temple building, but it's more of a complex of buildings with some great names. OK, the gateway is just called The Gateway, but that takes you into the Permanent Resident Compound. This is really another gateway decorated with giant dragons. The central path is called the Forest of Steles and takes you into the heart of the complex. Even this is special because on both sides of the path there are tablets and headstones in honour of famous monks and martial artists. As I read their names, I tried to imagine what some of these great fighting monks looked like.

Parts of the temple have been knocked down and rebuilt several times but other parts are original. Yanli took me into a beautifully decorated hall called Devajara Hall.

It had statues of two really scary warriors called Hum and Haw at the entrance. The gateway had been rebuilt in 1983, but it still looked really old. In the Devajara Hall there were many statues, the most famous of them being the Four Heavenly Kings. They didn't look like heavenly kings, they looked like really angry Chinese bouncers, but maybe that's just a cultural thing, a club culture thing.

Most of the halls had statues, and statues to protect the statues. Like all good temples in China there was also a Drum Tower and a Bell Tower. They are like watchtowers rising high above the other buildings.

There were two halls that I really wanted to see, and Yanli left them both until last. It was as if she knew that they would be special to me.

The first was the Thousand Buddha Hall. This hall has a very famous painting that is made up of lots of smaller paintings showing some of the most important Arhats, or elders, ever to have lived. But what I really love about this hall is the floor. It still has its original bricks, with lots of worn places made by the monks as they practised their kung fu. In some of the ancient dents you can almost see the shape of their toe prints. I went and put my feet in some of these prints and did a bit of practice myself to carry on the tradition.

The second hall was the Baiyi Hall. If ever there was a place I had wanted to see, this was it. I had been to Ethiopia, I had been to Palestine, Babylon and Graceland, but this was the only pilgrimage that I had ever really, and I mean really, wanted to make. I had heard about it as a child. My first karate teacher had told me about it, I had seen posters of it, and I had seen it in many martial arts books and films. Now I was stepping into it—little old me, big old it.

Yanli waited outside. She knew this

was a very meaningful personal and spiritual moment for me. Like all of the halls we had seen in the temple, it was smaller than you would expect. In the centre was a large statue of the Buddha sitting in the lotus position with incense burning in front of him, but I was more interested in the walls. These were covered with large frescoes, or paintings, which are the earliest known works of art showing monks practising kung fu. At first the monks look quite comical, fat and overdressed and not at all like the martial artists of today. But when you look more closely they tell us a lot about the development and the practice of kung fu.

The frescoes show clearly what the buildings looked like all those years ago and how kung fu training was carried out, with a mixture of weapons and empty hand fighting. What impressed me more than anything else was that the fighters came from many nationalities. The paintings tell us that the temple was an international meeting place and such a coming together of cultures represented everything I believe in. I wanted to worship here, but I also wanted to show the images to people back in London who say multiculturalism can't work, and say, 'Look, Shaolin kung fu fighters from all over the world have come together for hundreds of years. This tradition is still going strong, so get your act together. There is beauty and strength in diversity.'

*　　　*　　　*

I lost track of time and so wasn't sure how long I spent in there but I came out a new person. I was going to carry on the Shaolin tradition.

Chapter Eleven

The Forest of Pagodas

We thanked the monk at The Gateway, who was still eating pizza, and we left the Shaolin Temple.

'Can I show you something?' Yanli asked me.

We walked out of the temple and turned right. Rising up in front, and on both sides of us, were large pillars of all shapes and sizes.

'This is the Forest of Pagodas,' said Yanli.

I had thought a pagoda was a building, but these were giant decorated stones on top of the graves of famous monks, abbots and Arhats. When you saw them from the road, the pagodas almost looked like dark trees nestled in the company of their green, living relatives. The forest was huge, with more than 250 pagodas.

'How many more?' I kept asking as we walked round.

'More,' was always the reply.

The pagodas have always been difficult to count. During the Qing Dynasty, the emperor sent 500 of his guards to count them. They counted and recounted but kept coming up with different numbers. The guards told the emperor that it was impossible to count the number of pagodas in the forest.

'Why?' asked the emperor.

'Because it really is a forest,' they replied. 'The pagodas just keep growing. Some may even be moving.'

The first pagoda was made for an Indian monk called Sakamuni, and his is the tallest. The pagodas have Buddhist holy writing carved on them and a history of the life of the deceased, but in China not everything is as it seems at first. Near the gate there was a large pagoda that looked extremely old. As I walked around it admiring the kung fu fighters using sticks and knives and doing various exercises, I saw a carving of a laptop computer, a digital camera and then a jumbo jet. No one could explain why these modern elements had been added to the pagoda, and I could see some people thinking this showed a lack of respect, but after giving it a few moments to sink in I began to think they were rather sweet. Well, they put a smile on my face anyway.

*   *   *

As Yanli and I were leaving the Forest of Pagodas, I heard a voice calling.

'Hey, Birmingham guy. Come here.'

I looked up to see Fat Thumb. He was waving me over.

'I'm busy,' I shouted.

'Come here. Just for a minute. I've got something to tell you.'

I walked over to him.

'What's up, man?'

'I have something to tell you,' Fat Thumb said. 'The early worm gets the chicken.'

'What does that mean?' I asked.

'It means the late dog gets nothing.'

'What are you on, and what did you call me over for?' I was getting irritated again.

'You told me that you were sick of learning from second-rate kung fu teachers and you wanted the real thing.'

'That's right,' I replied.

'Have you been having any lessons?'

'Yes.'

'And what are they like?'

'They're OK. I train hard, it gets painful sometimes, but that's cool.'

'That's not cool,' he shouted. 'This no pain, no gain thing is rubbish. These teachers fool you into believing that if you are working hard and feeling pain you are doing well, but that's not true. You're wasting your money. Here's the deal. For the small fee of one hundred yuan a lesson, I will teach you the art of Smelly Finger, also known as the art of fighting without thinking.'

'You're talking rubbish,' I said.

Fat Thumb looked at me from head to toe and then from toe to head. 'How is your silence?'

'How is my silence?' I said. 'I dunno. I haven't spoken to it for a while.'

'You must find your silence and speak to it,' he said. 'You came for kung fu training, but you have not trained at all until you have trained with me.'

'I have started my lessons with Iron Breath. He knows his stuff and it's going OK,' I said.

Fat Thumb started doing that half smiling and half frowning thing with his face that wise people do.

'I know of Iron Breath. His kung fu is no good. It is like water in paper— it leaks. It is like bird in cage, it is limited. It is like a doctor with no brain.'

'What does that mean? I asked.

'That means the doctor is dead and cannot make you better. I will be your teacher and your power will increase. The Smelly Finger style cannot be bettered. It is beyond Shaolin. It is beyond Birmingham.'

'I've already paid for my lessons and I only have a short time left in Shaolin. Thanks for offering to help, but I'm sure I'll be fine.'

He handed me a book that he had been holding. It was a paperback, not very long, but old.

'I have bought something for you.'

'What's this about?' I asked.

Fat Thumb went all serious.

'These are the secrets of my style. Very few people have read this book. It is only for the chosen few, and you have been chosen.'

The book felt very fragile. I opened it slowly.

'It's all in Chinese,' I said, as if he

didn't know.

'That doesn't matter,' he said. 'Just having the book with you will do you good. Take it.'

'Are you sure?'

'Yes, I'm sure,' he said.

I was beginning to feel nervous. I didn't want to owe him anything. Actually, I didn't want to see him again for the rest of my life.

'Look, I can't read the book and I don't need the book.'

'Don't worry,' he said. 'The book can read you.'

'OK, if you insist. I don't see the point, but if you insist. I really have to go now,' I said, walking away. 'Thanks anyway.'

*　　*　　*

I kept the book to myself until we were in the taxi heading back, then I took it out.

'I have been given this book,' I said to Yanli. 'Could you please tell me what it's about?'

She took it from me very carefully. As she looked at it, her expression changed.

She looked up at me. 'Benjamin. Where did you get this from?'

'The guy with the long beard gave it to me. What's it about?'

'This really is something,' she said.

'What is it?' I said.

'Can I borrow it?' she asked.

'Yanli,' I whispered urgently. 'What is it about?'

'It's about soya,' she said.

'Soya?'

'Yes, soya.'

'What's soya got to do with anything?' I said, baffled.

Yanli looked down at the book. 'I don't know, but it's really interesting. I didn't know that soya beans are so useful. It says here that there are hundreds of different types of soya bean and as well as using them for food they can be used to make clothes, rope, containers, even lipstick.'

'Why would he want to give me that?' I said, thinking aloud.

'I don't know,' said Yanli, handing the book back to me, 'but it's very interesting. I'd like to read it when you have finished with it.'

Yanli dropped me at the hotel. I was left with not much to do but look at a book about the soya bean in a language that I couldn't read. Being a vegan means that I turn to the humble soya bean for many things. So a bit more information about the bean could have been useful, but I just couldn't work out why that weird guy, Fat Thumb, would want to give me this knowledge. I ended up sending a couple of emails, watching Comrade Mao's Long March on TV and practising my kung fu moves.

Chapter Twelve

Cash Money

The next morning I was woken by someone knocking on the door of my hotel room. I looked at my watch. It was 10 a.m. Knowing that Iron Breath always turned up at midday, I thought it was the cleaners.

'Come back later,' I shouted, but the knocking continued.

'Please. I'm sleeping. Could you please come back later?'

The knocking didn't stop.

'I said later.'

It looked as if the knocking was never going to end so I jumped up and looked through the spyhole in the door. Looking back at me was Iron Breath.

'Iron Breath,' I shouted. 'What are you doing here so early? Wait a minute.'

I ran to the bathroom, splashed some water over me, quickly put on the tracksuit that I trained in and opened the door.

'Iron Breath. Sorry. You're early.'

Iron Breath was a man of little emotion at the best of times and this wasn't even the best of times. He just stared at me as if he was going to kill me.

'What's the problem?' I said.

'Money,' he replied.

'Money. You need some money.'

As I was speaking, I was waving my hands about. I hoped it would help him understand me. It works when he's teaching me.

It was no good. He just stood there saying, 'Money.'

'OK,' I said. 'I know what to do, I'll call Yanli.'

I explained to Yanli what was happening and gave Iron Breath the phone so that she could speak to him.

They finished talking and Iron

Breath passed me the phone.

'What's up, Yanli?'

'He wants some more money,' she said.

'More money? What for? I paid him what he asked for up front, I've had no extra lessons, nothing has changed. Why does he want more?'

'I know, Benjamin. I told him this but he just said he wants more. I can't really argue with him, he's my elder. It would be disrespectful.'

'But Yanli, forget his age, he's wrong. You can't let anyone do anything to you just because they are old.' I was angry.

'Benjamin,' she said, 'calm down. He is only asking for another three thousand yuan.'

'Another three thousand yuan? He can forget it.'

As I was saying all this, Iron Breath was looking at me as cool as ice. He just looked at me and breathed. I, meanwhile, couldn't understand why Yanli didn't share my outrage.

'So why can't you say something to him on my behalf?' I went on. 'Tell him I've got no more money to give him, and we should just carry on like before because a deal is a deal.'

'OK, Benjamin. Let me speak to him.'

This was it. I expected something to kick off, and I didn't care in what language it would happen, but no, they just talked on in a civilised manner and then Iron Breath handed me the phone again.

'Benjamin,' said Yanli, 'he still says he wants three thousand yuan more.'

'What's come over him?

'I don't know. He doesn't want to talk about anything with me, he just wants more money,' she said.

'But I only have three more lessons left with him. I know the form already. We're just doing some extra fighting techniques and some breathing techniques. I could just stop now and go home.'

'I know you could, and I told him that but he didn't say anything.'

I huffed and I puffed, and I said, 'All right then. He can have his money.'

I just couldn't see the point of arguing any more. I thought I was paying too much already, but it was important to me to use all the time I had with the best teacher, and he was the best teacher. I didn't want to go home and regret it.

'Give him the phone,' said Yanli.

They spoke for a while and then Iron Breath handed the phone back to me.

'He wants you to pay him now,' said Yanli nervously.

'Pay him *now*? I've just got out of bed, and anyway I haven't got any Chinese money left. I need to change some money.'

'There's no need to get excited,' she said calmly. 'Just go downstairs, change some money, pay him, and he'll carry on with the lessons.'

'Yanli, are you working with him on this? Are you working with him to rip me off?'

'No,' she said. 'I just want peace.'

'I want peace too. I'll go and get the money now. Talk to you later.'

I went down to the reception with Iron Breath following me. I felt rather strange asking the receptionist to change some money for me when Iron Breath was standing so close behind me. I felt like explaining to the person behind the desk that he was actually a friend and not holding a gun to my back. But that was the least of my problems.

'Sir,' said the receptionist, 'we cannot change your money. We do not change pounds.'

'What have you got against pounds?' I asked.

'Nothing, sir. We just don't change them.'

I looked towards a board on the wall showing all the exchange rates.

'But you have the rates up there,' I said, pointing to the board.

'Sorry, sir,' she said blankly.

Call me old-fashioned, call me British, but I have this thing. When I travel, I hate using what people call American dollars, or what I call USA dollars. I want to use the currency of the country that I'm in, or the currency of my home country. Then, as I looked up at the board, I remembered I had a few USA dollars.

'OK,' I said. 'Can you change some American dollars for me?'

'No,' she replied. 'We don't change money here.'

I couldn't believe what I was hearing.

'What do you mean you don't change money? There's a currency chart there and you call yourself an international hotel. Have I missed something?'

'Sorry, sir. We don't change money. You can try the bank.'

Well, I couldn't try the bank because it was a holiday and the banks were closed, but as I walked around the reception area talking to myself with Iron Breath following me, I was stopped by a man in his late twenties.

'What's the matter, man? Do you have a problem here?' he said, sounding like a New York cop.

'I can't change any money,' I said. 'I'm in an international hotel where they display the currency exchange rates of twenty countries in their reception, but they say they don't change money. Go to the bank, they say, but no banks are open. So what do I do?'

'Come with me,' he said.

'Can you change money?'

'No,' he said, 'but I know a woman who can.'

'Can I bring my Shifu?' I asked, looking towards Iron Breath.

'No problem. What's your name?'

'I'm Benjamin. My teacher's called

Iron Breath. He doesn't say much. And yours?'

'John.'

'It's OK,' I said, 'you can tell me your Chinese name, I'll try to pronounce it and if I can't, just correct me.'

'John's my name,' he said. 'My family are Christians so my parents gave me a Christian name. There are lots of Christians here. You know that, don't you? Because I've heard that outside China some people don't know that there are Christians here. I know a Paul and a Matthew, and a Mary, but she's no saint,' he added with a grin and a wink.

*   *   *

John had never left China but spoke English with a very strong American accent. He had studied English at school and university but his accent came from watching films from the USA.

As we drove, he told me about his big dilemma. He loved his car, it drove wonderfully, it was reliable, his mother loved it, his friends loved it, but there was a problem. The car was Japanese and he hated the Japanese. When I asked him why he hated the Japanese, he gave me the reply so many Chinese people had given me.

'Nanking,' he said.

He was speaking about what is known as the Rape of Nanking. Nanking is now called Nanjing. In December 1937 the invading Japanese army went into Nanking and commited one of the most terrible crimes of all time. Over six weeks some 80,000 women were raped and many of them were then mutilated or murdered. Over 30,000 people were killed. Most Japanese people do not know the truth about the horrors that took place as many Japanese history books simply say that there was a battle in Nanking, some heavy stuff happened, and they won. No Japanese government has apologised for what happened at Nanking, but because the events were so well photographed and filmed (by the Japanese) Chinese people of all ages will never forget this dreadful moment in history.

'I hate the Japanese,' said John. 'They make me sick. I want to kill them, but they make really good cars, and computer games, and motorbikes, and DVD players, and . . .'

He went on for quite a while about all the great things made in Japan so I just had to say what I did.

'You sound like you love the Japanese to me.'

'I hate them.'

At this point I gave my much used speech about forgiveness. I told him that most Japanese don't know what really happened in Nanjing, just like Chinese people don't really know what happened in Tibet. I explained that most people from the USA don't know what really happened in Japan, and most white people don't really understand what happened to black people in slavery, but we must move forward.

Then I paused and said, 'If black people hated every nation that did bad things to them, we would hate everyone.'

'I guess you're right, but it's a difficult one to get over,' he said seriously.

*　　　*　　　*

Soon John and I arrived at a shop that sold arts and crafts. Iron Breath sat on the back seat like a statue of the Buddha while John and I went in. Inside John did a bit of whispering to a stern-looking woman behind the counter and I changed four hundred pounds into yuan at a very poor exchange rate. As we were saying goodbye, John told me another problem he had with the Japanese.

'Girls,' he said. 'Japanese girls. They look really nice, man.'

Chapter Thirteen

Acid Rain Takeaway

The next day things were back to normal. Iron Breath turned up at my hotel on time and worked me hard. I knew that I should be getting used to this level of training, and that my body would adapt, but in reality it was getting harder and harder.

Much of the lesson was spent doing nothing—doing nothing in the horse stance. The horse stance improves the strength of your legs. It's simple to do. Just stand with your knees bent and your legs well apart as if you were sitting on a horse. After a minute you will want to get up, but you must stay, and it gets more difficult. When you really feel that this should come to an end, you are told to go lower. The lower you get the more painful it is.

This is what Iron Breath did to me, and when I was as low as I could get he took two cups from the table, filled them with water and put them on my thighs. As I struggled to stay low, and to stay still, he sat in front of me, with a wise smile on his face and said, 'Good. Very good.'

*   *   *

When the session was over, I called Yanli. I wanted her to suggest to Iron Breath that I have a day off. I needed a day to recover, a day when maybe I could get out and see some of the countryside, but Iron Breath's reply (in Chinese) was, 'No way.'

That's what Yanli told me he said. He also said, 'If he wants a day off, he can have a day off when the training is over. If he needs a day off now, the course will finish here and now and there will be no refund.'

As Yanli was telling me this, I was looking at Iron Breath standing right in front of me. He just didn't seem like the same man whose words were being spoken to me. Who was he anyway? I knew nothing about him, nothing. I didn't know where he came from. I didn't know if he had ever been in love. I didn't know if he liked football. I didn't even know if he liked me. All I knew was that he was a good teacher who liked to be well paid for his services.

'It's up to you,' said Yanli.

'Forget it,' I replied.

I handed the phone to Iron Breath and when they had spoken for a while he handed it back to me.

'Benjamin,' she said, 'he said you are a good student but you must train harder. He said from now on he will not do warm-up exercises with you. He will expect you to do them before he comes, and he will train you harder than before. He was training you at a child's level before, now he will train you at a man's level. If you complain, you must go home.

He said this is kung fu, not dancing.'

'I understand,' I said.

Iron Breath went home and I sat on my bed wondering if he was joking. I got back on the phone to Yanli.

'Yanli, tell me straight. Is he joking?'

'No,' said Yanli. 'He may seem strange, but no.'

We arranged to meet up later that evening and I fell asleep.

*   *   *

I woke up late in the afternoon weak and hungry, so I decided to make the trip up the hill to the Yong Tai Temple restaurant. The moment I stepped out of the taxi there was a frenzy of activity.

Two girls stood at the entrance and it seemed like their job was simply to bow to me. Another girl showed me to my seat, while another girl drew back the chair for me to sit in. At the same time different girls got me a menu, some water, some tea, brought me a warm towel, and brought me a little fluffy dragon for good luck.

It was as if they had been waiting for me before they sprang into action. They remembered to bring me an English menu and not a Chinese one; they remembered that I liked the air conditioning turned off; and they remembered to bring me knives, forks and spoons because I couldn't use chopsticks. One thing they didn't remember, or chose not to remember, was that I liked small portions. I love my vegan food but I really don't like eating a lot, and I also don't like wasting food.

The Chinese eat big. It amazes me how much some of them can eat and still stay so small. If a Chinese person is in a restaurant and they think they've had enough, they will not leave and allow the food to be thrown away. They will ask for the

Dabao or a doggy bag as it's sometimes called. It is considered normal to take home what's left over. It's something that I think we should all do. I always think it's wrong that most uneaten food ends up in rubbish bins or down drains.

*　　　*　　　*

I ate as much as I could, took my little doggy bag and said goodbye to my kind hosts. When I got outside the restaurant, I found the taxi driver who had taken me there waiting for me.

'We go back,' he said.

'No,' I replied. 'I want to walk back.'

'No, no,' he said. 'Too far.'

'Don't worry about me, I'll be OK,' I said as I set off.

It was downhill all the way. It feels so much longer when you're doing it on foot, and this was just the road down from the temple to the main road. Near the end of the temple road I heard a car coming down behind me so I began to walk as close to the edge of the road as possible but the car slowed down and drove alongside me.

It was the taxi again. The driver shouted out of the window, 'OK, sir. Good walk. Now I take you to hotel.'

'No, I told you, I want to walk.'

'It is far, sir.'

'I know it's far, but I want to walk. Please leave me alone.'

'OK,' he said, and he drove off.

It was a long walk. I walked for about two kilometres before I came to my favourite place with the kung fu kids. There were schools on both sides of the road with hundreds of young boys and girls practising their moves. If I had another shot at education, I'd study religious beliefs, but if I had another shot at being a child, I'd be a kung fu kid, in a kung fu school, in China. But I would come home for holidays. There's nothing quite like Blackpool in the summer.

I went on walking and checking out the schools and it began to drizzle. But the falling rain was no problem. I kept walking, wondering what was going through the minds of these young people, and what they thought of me looking on. I could see that many of them were being distracted by me so I never stayed outside any one school for too long.

When I stopped at a street stall to buy some iced tea, the taxi driver pulled up next to me again.

'Are you ready now, sir?' he asked.

'No,' I replied grumpily, 'and I'll never be ready. I want to walk. I like walking. These feet were made for walking. Walking, that's what I do.'

I thought he got the message that time. He sped off towards the town and I got my tea and went on my way. Soon after, I came across a group of boys and girls who had finished their classes and were taking some time out. They came up to me looking at my dreadlocks and discussing if they were real or not. I hadn't suddenly learnt how to understand Chinese, by the way, I just knew that this was the usual starting point for discussions about my locks.

I was beginning to feel like a UFO that had landed, until one boy pointed to me and said, 'Manchester United.'

'No,' I said. 'Aston Villa.'

'Aston Villa no good,' he said. 'Manchester United.'

Just then two girls stepped forward.

'Me, she, Aston Villa,' said one of the girls.

'Very good,' I replied.

'Yes,' she went on. 'Up the Villa.'

'Up the Villa,' I replied. Here I was, at the home of kung fu, with people who could well be the kung fu masters of the future, and we were talking about which English football team we supported. This wasn't right.

'You want to be kung fu monk?' I asked.

There were blank stares from all of them, so I tried something else. The Chinese words for 'Buddha bless you'.

'Er me tuo fo.'

'No, no,' said one of the boys. 'Not er me tuo fo.'

I pointed to him, did a kung fu hand movement and said, 'You, er me tuo fo?'

'No. Me Li Lianjie,' he replied.

'Li Lianjie,' I said. 'I know him. He's very good.'

Li Lianjie is the Chinese name for Jet Li, a big kung fu film star. He was also a student at one of the many schools around the Shaolin Temple, and starred in a classic film called *Shaolin Temple*. Most of the young people training at these schools have no wish to live the lonely life of a monk. They want to be movie stars, they want to make it big in Chinese films and then go on to Hollywood, or to be bodyguards for the rich and famous so they can mix with the movie stars.

I was just about to tell them how important their culture was and why some traditions should be kept alive when it started to pour with rain. The kids said goodbye and ran off.

My dreadlocks and my doggy bag of food got soaked with the heavy, polluted rain. There was nowhere to hide and all I could do was to start walking in the direction of my hotel. It was miserable, but help was at hand, and it came in the form of that same taxi driver who had taken me to the restaurant.

'You want taxi now, sir?' he shouted.

'Yes,' I said, defeated. 'I want taxi now.'

He drove me back in complete silence but I could tell that he was a happy man, twenty yuan richer than the last time I saw him.

Chapter Fourteen

Showtime

In my hotel room I had just about dried off and changed my clothes when Yanli phoned.

'I'm downstairs, on the second floor. I'll wait by the lift,' she said.

I made my way to the lift and when I got to the second floor the door opened and I was greeted by something quite unexpected. Yanli was waiting for me, and there was a full-scale disco underway. This wasn't a rave or a club night: this was a good old-fashioned disco, Chinese style.

'I thought you would like something different,' said Yanli.

'This is different all right, but the same as well.'

'What do you mean?' asked Yanli.

'It reminds me of the type of disco they used to have in Britain years ago.'

We sat down and began to drink soft drinks to the sounds of Bucks Fizz, Abba, Boney M and the Village People. Graceful young girls and tipsy, middle-aged men filled the dance floor. After a while the music stopped. Yanli quickly sat up straight.

'This is what I've been waiting for,' she said excitedly.

Everybody was excited. People ran around picking up microphones, a large screen slowly came down from the ceiling, and soon the place was turned into a giant karaoke machine.

I found the whole thing quite interesting in a strange way. That so many people wanted to step forward and sing along to pop songs, alone or in small groups, was impressive. They struggled to sing in English, but they were all enjoying themselves and everyone relished the clapping at the end of each song. The singers were out of tune and they were out of time, but they were happy.

As one of the songs ended, Yanli put her handbag on my lap and said, 'This is me.'

She stood in the centre of the floor and let the words of that karaoke classic, *I Will Survive*, ring out. She sang it with feeling, she sang it in time, she sang it in tune, and she sang it with passion. She danced, she did hand movements, she gave it all that she had and I actually wanted more. But when the song was over she returned to our table, took her bag and picked up her drink as if nothing had happened.

'That was good,' I said truthfully. 'Do you sing anything else?'

'I don't need to sing anything else,' she said. 'That says it all.'

Well, I couldn't argue with that. It is the most-sung karaoke song of all time, and it did really seem to mean something to her, but she would say nothing more. Like many Chinese, Yanli didn't give much away. The British have the stiff upper lip. The Chinese have the stiff upper eyebrow.

*   *   *

We were happily watching more karaoke singers when my worst nightmare happened. A group of people were standing around our table. At first I thought they had come to talk about whether my dreadlocks were real or not, but soon, with a little help from Yanli, I realised that it was much worse than that. They wanted me to sing.

One of them could just about speak English.

'We want you to sing for us. What is your song?' he said.

'No, I don't sing and I don't have a song.I just like to watch.'

'No, you must sing,' the spokesman

for the group said. 'You like *Billy Jean*, Michael Jackson? Michael Jackson is very good for you.'

'Michael Jackson is no good for me,' I replied.

'You like Lionel Richie?'

'Never heard of him,' I lied.

'Ah,' he said. 'I know. *Do You Feel My Love*. He got hair like you.'

He meant the song by Eddy Grant, of course. I was having none of it, but it's hard when you're surrounded by nice people with stiff upper eyebrows chanting, 'Sing, sing.'

'No, no,' I shouted.

'Sing, sing,' they chanted.

'No, no,' I shouted as I began to think of an excuse, but then Yanli joined in. On the wrong side.

'Go on, Benjamin. Sing for them.'

'Whose side are you on?' I asked. 'You should be backing me up. Get me out of here. I'm not gonna make a fool of myself.'

'So you think I was making a fool of myself?' she said. 'Who do you think you are? Do you think you are better than us?'

'Now, now, Yanli, don't take it personally. I don't think you made a fool of yourself. You were really good, and I definitely don't think I'm better than you. I just don't do karaoke.'

'But you are a performer. You are always on stage.'

'But I do anti-war poems, I do poems about how we must put an end to greed and overthrow tyranny, and form a decent society based on the organic vegan way of life. I don't do Eddy Grant songs.'

'Please,' she begged. 'It would mean so much to the people here. They don't ask for much, and you would make them so happy if you agreed to sing.'

It was hard to say no when she put it like that.

'OK,' I said, 'I'll do it.'

I took the microphone and headed for the centre of the floor. The video began to play and I began to sing.

I felt terrible. I had to force the words of the Eddy Grant song from my mouth, but the crowd loved it. I wouldn't dance but I nodded my head to help keep time and they thought that was cool. I died on stage that night, but luckily there was no one from the British media to record or report it.

Chapter Fifteen

Temple Time

The next few days were pretty cool. I just did as I was told. I woke up late every morning, I ate a banana, I did my training with Iron Breath, I had some muesli, I fell asleep. I woke up, I went to the Yong Tai Temple to eat and then I went home, sometimes stopping off to watch the kung fu kids training. I steered clear of the karaoke hall, although I had been invited back by people who had seen me sing.

*   *   *

On my last training day I woke up nice and early, happy that at last I was on Chinese time. I had learnt a lot and this was the day I wanted to show Iron Breath how good I was. I did some stretches and had a large bowl of muesli and a banana, before sitting down to check my emails.

The first email I opened brought me bad news. A friend of mine called Malik had been arrested. According to the police he was going to blow the whole country up, and with the help of his dentist and a man who once sold him a book he was going to set up a Muslim state in Britain with its capital in Aston, Birmingham.

I opened another email and it was from Malik's wife, begging me for help. She wanted me to use my contacts to get him freed. She didn't realise that I was in China, and anyway, like many others she thought I had more influence than I did.

There was nothing I could do. Not only was I 18,000 kilometres away, it was also 9 a.m. Chinese time and 2 a.m. in Birmingham. I had to put the problem in a corner of my mind and get on with the rest of the day.

I did some more stretching, some

light kung fu practice and some quiet meditation, and then I waited for Iron Breath to arrive. He was right on time, but Yanli was with him. My heart sank as this could only mean another problem.

'Good morning, and what's wrong?' I asked.

'Nothing,' said Yanli.

'So why are you here?'

'Because Iron Breath wants me to explain something to you,' she replied.

'OK. What is it and how much will it cost?'

'It will cost you nothing. It's just a change of plan for today. As it is your last day, Iron Breath wants to take you to practise with the Chinese students in the Shaolin Temple.'

I was so excited I hugged Yanli. She blushed but didn't stop me. I went to hug Iron Breath but he just seemed to hold me off with his energy.

'OK. Thank him for me, Yanli,' I said, 'and tell him I think he's cool.'

Yanli handed me a package she was holding.

'What's this?' I asked.

'It's a kung fu suit. You must wear it.'

'I'll wear it,' I said. 'I'll wear anything. I'll train naked. I just want to train in the Shaolin Temple, on the very spot where some of the greatest fighting monks in all history have trained. The place where Bodhidharma the Zen original breathed the mystic chi, the place where kung fu was born, that's where I want to be.'

'Put the suit on,' she said.

I did and soon we were on our way in a taxi. When we arrived at the temple, I was taken to a large courtyard where nothing was happening. We just stood there looking at an empty space, then suddenly about a hundred students marched in, dressed in bright orange kung fu suits just like mine.

They took up their positions, like

soldiers on parade, leaving space in the middle for one. Iron Breath pointed to the space. It was for me. I nervously went and took up my position. The other students did not look at me. They were all concentrating and looking straight ahead. Then it struck me. This was no game; these students were serious and they were probably all very good at what they did, so I mustn't let them down.

As we started to do stretches and warm-up exercises, I realised that nobody was going to make it easy for me because I couldn't speak Chinese, but I was warmed up already, and I was a good follower. Once the warm-up exercises were done everyone stood to attention as the Shifu performed the form for us. When the kung fu teacher had finished, he stood to attention and shouted the command for us to start.

Quickly I found a weakness in my moves. I was so used to performing at my own speed that I found it difficult to keep up with the speed of one hundred other students. The other thing was that the arrest of my Muslim friend Malik was on my mind and I felt guilty. Here I was worrying about getting a few kung fu moves right, and he was in some unknown place being questioned under the so-called Prevention of Terrorism Act. But what could I do? I kept asking myself. I had to concentrate and get through this.

*　　　*　　　*

I managed the form but I knew I hadn't done as well as I could do. I looked towards Iron Breath. His stiff upper eyebrow wasn't giving anything away, but I knew that my kicks were lazy and my stances were too high.

The Shifu gave a bit of a lecture that I didn't understand and we went through it all again. This time he walked among us. As he walked, he would correct the students' postures by twisting their limbs or kicking them into place. It looked painful. When he came to me, he watched me for a while but did nothing, which I thought was a good sign, but as he walked away he gently pushed me from behind to show me that my stance was incorrect. I stumbled a little but soon steadied myself and continued.

It was like training in heaven, but I had to stay focused. I would catch glimpses of Yanli and Iron Breath but I ignored them. Thoughts of Malik in custody drifted into my mind but I ignored them. Then, for some strange reason, I began to wonder who was in the *Big Brother* house. I had to put aside this evil thought and tell myself I was training on sacred ground. Everything had to be pushed aside to focus on the kung fu, but this is all part of it. You have to block out all other thoughts and get mind, body and breath working together. I think I just about did it.

The Shifu gave another short speech and then we got ready to do the form again. I glanced at Yanli and she raised a finger, and so I guessed this was the last time. As we began, the teacher walked towards me and Iron Breath joined him. They both watched me intently as I went through the form, ignoring the others. This made me worry more, but I knew the key was to keep relaxed, stay focused and feel every move that I made. And I did. It all seemed to come together quite well, and when I had finished Iron Breath and the Shifu bowed to each other, and Iron Breath gave what I thought was the beginnings of a smile, just enough to let me know that he wasn't unhappy.

When it was over, the students marched out as quickly as they had marched in. I went over to see Yanli. She was alone.

'Where's Iron Breath?' I asked.

'He just said he had to go,' she replied.

'Is he angry with me?'

'No,' she said hastily. 'Didn't you see? He almost smiled.'

'Yeah. You saw that too?'

'Yes, I saw it. I think he just had to go away. He wants me to thank you for your hard work and he wishes you the best for the rest of your life.'

'That's nice,' I said. 'I'm pleased that he cares about the rest of my life but it would have been nice to say goodbye to him in person.'

'I know,' said Yanli, 'but you have to understand, he is not very sentimental. He's done what you wanted him to do, you've done what he wanted you to do, so now it's over. You take your different roads in life.'

As we walked out of the temple, I heard someone calling me.

'Benjamin! Mr Benjamin!'

I looked around and saw Fat

Thumb walking up behind me. Yanli walked on and I waited for Fat Thumb to catch up with me.

'So what do you know?' he asked.

'I know some things and I don't know other things,' I replied. 'What do you know?'

'You are dressed for kung fu. Are you ready to study with me?'

'My studying here is finished for now. I leave tomorrow,' I said.

'So now you think you are a kung fu expert?'

'No,' I said. 'I didn't say that, but I'm leaving with more knowledge, wisdom and understanding than I had when I came here.'

'You have knowledge, but do you have the High Rise Mind, and do you know the difference between the Big Rum and the Big Rum?

'What are you on about, man? Do I have a High Rise Mind? What's the High Rise Mind? And, if you're so full of wisdom, you tell me what the difference is between the Big Rum and the Big Rum.'

'Now we're getting deep. This is true wisdom. The answer is . . .' He stared into the distance.

'Come on, then,' I said. 'You don't know, do you?'

'I have all the answers,' he said. 'The difference is one Big Rum is first and the other Big Rum is not.'

I had had enough.

'I gotta go,' I said, stretching out my right hand for a shake. He just looked down at my hand, so I said, 'Goodbye. And I hope you can get it together, man. Whatever it is.'

I went over to Yanli and we began to walk away from the temple.

'Do you know that guy?' I asked.

'No one really knows him but I know some things about him. It's really sad. His parents come from Hong Kong but live in England.I think they come from Birmingham, where you come from.'

'I knew it,' I said. 'I knew he had a Brummie accent.'

'He comes from a very rich family,' Yanli continued. 'He went to an expensive school, and to one of the best universities in England, but when he left university something happened. We don't really know what, but it had something to do with him being told by other Chinese people that he wasn't Chinese enough. He couldn't speak Chinese. He didn't mix with Chinese people.

'Then he started reading anything he could about Chinese beliefs and religions. China became a special place for him, so he got a one-way ticket here. He believed he was a dead kung fu monk reborn. Fat Thumb can't fight. If you ask him to show you his kung fu, he just stands there and says that you're not wise enough to see it. Basically he's mad. He just lost it somewhere, and I think he may have lost it here.'

'That's a big shame,' I said, 'but I've seen it before. I've seen lots of black British people go to Africa because they see it as the great motherland, but when they get there they just can't cope with it. And I have to say, the Shaolin Temple that I've seen here is very different from the Shaolin Temple in the books and in the films. I had a different place in mind, but I can deal with this.'

'The true Shaolin Temple has gone,' said Yanli. 'This is a tourist attraction. Yes, there are some good kung fu teachers around, and there is some history here, but it's no longer a spiritual place, a place to think and be still. He won't be around for very long,' Yanli continued, as she pointed to Fat Thumb. 'He will wake up, break up, or simply move on, and then someone else will take his place. They come and go, just like the tourists really. People like him just stay for a little bit longer than the average tourist.'

It was all very sad really. I stopped and looked back and my last view of the great Shaolin Temple was one with Fat Thumb standing in front of the entrance picking his nose.

Yanli dropped me off at the hotel in a taxi. In saying goodbye she was a bit more emotional than Iron Breath but not much.

'Goodbye, and I hope you enjoyed your stay here and that you will come again.'

'Yeah. Goodbye,' I said. 'And if you're ever in England, give me a call. You have my number.'

She shook my hand and we parted. I wasn't expecting a leaving party but it was all a bit formal. I went to my hotel room, had a shower and sat at the telephone with my address book in hand.

I rang Malik's wife, Fatima, who told me how in the early hours of the morning the front door of their house was battered down by the police and her father-in-law was pushed down the stairs. Her mother-in-law was taken from the room she was praying in, and Malik was dragged out of bed and arrested. Fatima had not been told where he was being held.

I then rang my mother, just to tell her that I missed her. Then I spent the next two hours ringing around friends to make sure they had not been arrested and that they knew where to find help if they or any of their family were arrested. This was today's Britain. We were told that we were free to express our political and religious beliefs, but not, it seemed, if you were a Muslim or a friend of a Muslim.

Chapter Sixteen

Return of the Money Monk

The next morning I woke up early and packed, and waited for my taxi driver to take me from the hotel to the airport.

I had been in the check-in queue for less than ten minutes when I saw a sight I never thought I'd see again. Iron Breath and Yanli were heading my way.

Yanli was out of breath. Iron Breath was not.

'What's the matter? Have I done something wrong?' I said.

'I don't know what's happening,' said Yanli. 'Iron Breath just called me this morning and told me to take him to meet you here. I have no idea what it's about.'

'Well, you're here now. Ask him what's wrong.'

She spoke to him but he said nothing. He just stepped forward and stood right in front of me. I thought he was going to shoot me or blow me away with his iron breath. He reached into his robe and pulled out a parcel wrapped in Mickey Mouse wrapping paper and handed it to me.

'A present,' I said. 'Isn't that nice? You came all this way to give me a present.'

I bowed slightly and gave the Buddhist blessing, 'Er me tuo fo.'

I turned to Yanli. 'Thank him for me, please.'

'Open it,' she said.

I unwrapped the Mickey Mouse paper to find a bundle of money. I could tell by the rubber bands around the notes that these were the very same notes that I had paid Iron Breath with. Two distinct bundles. One from the first payment, and one from the second. Yanli was as surprised as me. She began speaking to him quickly and excitedly, then she turned to me.

'He said that all the money that you paid to him is there except one hundred and sixty yuan, which he used to buy the kung fu suit for you.'

'And he wants me to take it all back?' I said, in disbelief.

'Yes,' she said.

'Wow!' I said, amazed. 'But why?'

'It's a Chinese thing,' she said.

This is why I love China and the Chinese people. You never know what's just over the hill. Ancient tombs have computers carved into them; you think someone is working you to death when they are actually bringing new life to you; the person you think is ripping you off is just saving your money for you. They really know how to be cruel to be kind.

The check-in queue moved on.

'I think I have to go now,' I said. 'Please thank him from the bottom of my heart.'

'I will,' said Yanli.

I smiled, Yanli smiled, and then it happened. Iron Breath smiled. It was like a film. We said our goodbyes and went our different ways.

Then Yanli was running towards me with Iron Breath walking fast behind her.

'What's wrong now?' I said, puzzled once more.

'Iron Breath needs to ask you a favour.'

'Ask away,' I said.

'Can you give him some money for the taxi fare home?'

I laughed. 'Of course I can. Does he want his money back?'

'No,' she said. 'Just enough to cover the taxi fare.'

I gave him four hundred yuan. He bowed, and said, 'Er me tuo fo.'

Then they headed off, and I went through the gates of no return.

Chapter Seventeen

Back to Beijing

I slept on the plane all the way back to Beijing. A perfect flight. I began to think about Malik again so before unpacking in my hotel room in the Chinese capital I rang his wife, Fatima. There was good news. Malik had been released on bail and had to go back to the police station two weeks later. Like many arrests around that time the police had nothing on him. They were just trying to look as if they were really fighting a war on terror.

I had to leave for London the next day so after hearing the good news about Malik I decided I needed to do something I liked, and I went to the gym.

Zhao Bin—the hotel's gym team leader—was so pleased to see me back that she called all her staff to watch me work out again. They gave me time to warm up, and then Zhao Bin said, 'OK, Mr Shaolin, let us see some of your new moves.'

I duly performed my new form for them and they were delighted. My new form was three times as long as the old one and a lot more difficult, and they knew it.

'We're so proud of you,' said Zhao Bin. 'Everyone's talking about you.'

'Me?' I said, genuinely surprised.

'Yes, you. You come here with your fit body and show even the Chinese people kung fu. And everybody loves your hair. Everybody's talking about you, everyone. We hear that you are a great karaoke star too.'

'No, that's not right. I'm a revolutionary poet.'

'You are nice man.'

'Thanks,' I said, and they stepped back to watch me finish the rest of my workout.

I went back to my room and had a

143

shower, and as I was getting dressed the phone rang. I picked it up, and said, 'Hello,' but no one answered.

After about ten minutes there was a knock on my door. I couldn't believe it. It was Louise, the kissy kissy woman who had come into my room uninvited all those days ago. She just stepped past me and turned the television off.

'No excuses,' she said. 'I am ready for you now.'

'Please,' I said. 'Leave me alone.'

'You don't want to kiss me?' she said.

'I think you're very nice,' I replied, 'but I'm doing a monk thing at the moment. You know, no woman, no sex.'

'I think you are gay boy.'

'Let's not go over that again,' I said. 'I'm not a gay boy, but if that's what you need to give me a break I'll be a gay boy. Yes, yes, I'm gay, very, very gay.'

She walked up to me and pointed

144

in my face.

'I know you. You are famous man, I saw you on internet. You are famous.'

'I'm not really famous. If I was famous, you would have recognised me straight away. I'm just a well-known British poet.'

'Kiss me,' she demanded.

'I can't, but I can read you some poems,' I said.

She went very quiet. She walked over to the bed, lay right in the centre of it, and said, 'OK. Give me some poems, dark man.'

I read my poem *Dis Poetry* to her. She looked me in the eyes.

'Nice,' she said. 'Give me more.'

Then I read *Man to Man*, followed by *Naked*, and she wanted more, so for the next half-hour I read to her as if I was reading to a crowd of hundreds and all she could say was, 'Nice. More.'

When I had finished, she got up and walked to the door.

'Well, I guess this is goodbye,' I said.

I just wasn't sure what was going through her head. She looked me up and down, and then she opened the door. She stepped out of the door, looked me up and down again and began to walk away. As she walked, she waved, smiled and said, 'You good. Yes, you really good, dark man.'